SEAN PATRICK TAYL(
Literature from the Universi
musician and theatre artist i._____, ____ _____ _____ in medieval
and ancient literature through various continuing learning programs. His
translations of *Cyrano de Bergerac* and *A Doll's House* have been staged at
Seattle Shakespeare Company. His previous collection of poems, *A Cold
Day in Hell*, appeared as a chapbook in the Laguna Poets Series of The
Inevitable Press (1998).

WHAT FOREIGN SHORE

Poems based on the Odes of Horace

Sean Patrick Taylor

SilverWood

Published in 2019 by SilverWood Books

SilverWood Books Ltd
14 Small Street, Bristol, BS1 1DE, United Kingdom
www.silverwoodbooks.co.uk

ISBN 978-1-78132-934-4 (paperback)
ISBN 978-1-78132-959-7 (ebook)

British Library Cataloguing in Publication Data
A CIP catalogue record for this book is
available from the British Library

Page design and typesetting by SilverWood Books
Printed on responsibly sourced paper

FOR MY FATHER

Contents

Just a Word Before I Go

quae caret ora cruore nostro?

"What shore still lacks our blood?" That's the line of Horace, from the first poem of the second book of what is traditionally called the *Carmina* (the songs), which western classical scholarship has called the *Odes*, that first called out to me.

Odes are addressed to someone (if to some*thing*, they are called apostrophes). Quintus Horatius Flaccus, born in 65 BCE, was addressing his friend Pollio, who was writing a history on the civil wars between Octavian and Antony, in which Pollio took an active, if vacillating, part. Horace (as we call him), who also fought in the war, seems to be trying to dissuade him from this work, calling him back to what Horace felt was his more important mission: writing tragedies for the Roman stage.[1]

I think it was the resignation of the verse that engaged me: As if to say, "Why the hell do you want to waste your time writing of the mindless carnage of Roman killing Roman, when all of our history is up to our knees in blood, against every country on Earth?" By that time, Rome was shedding blood, and by no means more of its own than that of others, on every foreign shore in the known world.

---

1 We are indebted to Pollio that he didn't listen to his friend's advice. Though his history is lost, it formed the foundation for much of Plutarch's *Lives*, without which we would not have Shakespeare's *Julius Caesar* and *Antony and Cleopatra*.

But for Horace, such paroxysm of violence simply formed part of the weave of human experience—regrettable, no doubt, but no more to be blamed or sorrowed over than the fierce waves battering the west coast of Italy on the Tyrhennian sea. And so, his logic went, Pollio was wasting his time chronicling an event which was simply one advent of an endless repetition of a tragic human cycle, which he might better witness in poetic fiction, since human events simply reproduce eternal truths, spooling out endlessly over time.

That kind of fatalism might make for a poesy of brooding sorrow. But that's not our Horace. He seems to me to be sitting on a bench in his back garden, sipping good red wine from his cup, knowing well that his world is going to hell, but keeping a rather strained smile all the time. A true figure for our times.

Some time back, having made rough translations of all the *Odes*, I undertook to work a selection of them, the ones that really spoke to me, into finished verse. But quickly the translator's eternal dilemma presented itself, one I've confronted often over the years: Is the poem to remain anchored in the world of the original, or truly carried over into the present? I have in the past been a frequent advocate of the former, as I have seen some translators take extravagant liberties with their originals, too often (it seems to me) out of a condescending assumption that their readers are not up to negotiating the past on any level.

And yet, as I began work on the third in this volume, I questioned what resonance the reference to snow-covered Mt. Soracte might have for the modern reader, and even what relevance the poem's being addressed to one Thaliarchus might have for *me* (I had already substituted a figure from my own past for Pyrrha in 1.5). At the moment, I was looking out my window to the Olympic mountain range, it seemed to me that Mt. Constance might do just as well as Soracte, and that as long as I were describing an evening with a friend over wine, I might use as my model the very night before, where I shared a bottle and a dish of pears with a friend. The resulting poem retains Horace's wistful pleasure, at one remove, in knowing that, while the advance of time is inexorable, time remains for the young girl to be wooed in dim corners...rather as I had attempted, long ago, with the very woman with whom I was sharing the bottle, looking out at Mt. Constance. The new poem owed much to Horace, but was no longer situated in first-century BC Campania, but the Pacific Northwest in the present day—partly a poem of Horace, partly my own.

This was the course I adopted for the remainder of the project, to render the Horatian *Odes* into a new account: not quite translations, but variations on a traditional theme. Part of my warrant for this was my fear that retaining every original reference might ossify these beautiful poems into museum pieces. In any case, a faithful translation of the *Odes* has already been recently performed, by a more accomplished hand than my own.[2] The freedom to use the *Odes* as a point of excursus for a more immediate meditation on my own experiences, and on the world I inhabit, has provided much of the pleasure I've taken in the project. Some of the poems herein follow their originals very closely. Some carry over only portions of the originals (one, "Mourning," only two stanzas). Sometimes, especially in the case of the more fulsomely patriotic odes (I have not even bothered to include the notorious *dulce et decorum est pro patria mori*), I have subverted the original sense entirely.

Additionally, it will be immediately apparent to any reader familiar with the originals that I have not attempted to replicate Horace's original verse metrics, which he had adapted from earlier Greek lyric forms.

2 I refer the reader to Jeffrey H. Kaimowitz's elegant translation, *The Odes of Horace* (Johns Hopkins New Translations from Antiquity), 2008.

Classical verse forms, relying on syllabic quantity, cannot be easily adapted to English, which makes use of syllabic stress, even in informal speech. I have taken the opportunity to experiment with many verse forms—*terza rima*, villanelle, sonnet, sometimes simply blank verse. Yet since so many of the originals conform to the Sapphic pattern, which Horace associated with the Aeolian islands north of Sicily, I found myself increasingly adopting an English version of this all my own: three lines of iambic pentameter, followed by a short line of three stresses, often rhyming ABAB.

Exigi monumentum. Now that the work is finished, I can only hope that it may give as much pleasure to a select coterie of readers that it has to me in the performance. I depart from Horace in his epilogue, in which he claims the immortality that his *Odes* have so deservedly conferred on him. I make no such claim for these poems, since poetry no longer seems a viable path to fame for anyone—and in any case, they are only partly mine to begin with. I can only express my gratitude to this genial man from so long ago, with whom I feel I would have got along well, for granting the urge to contemplate for a time the beauty of simple things, like breaking the seal on a jar of very old wine. Yes, tomorrow comes sorrow, tomorrow comes ruin. All the more reason to plunder this day.

Ce n'est l'air des Latins ny le mont Palatin,
Qui ores (mon Ronsard) me fait parler Latin,
Changeant à l'estranger mon naturel langage.

Joachim du Bellay, *Regrets*, 10.1-4

Spring
(1.4)

Hard Winter melts with welcome turn of Spring:
    With winches fishermen draw dried hulls up the beach;
The herd's no longer warmed in stables, the peasant
    by the fire, the meadow no more grey with frost.

Now Venus leads her dance beneath a hanging moon,
    And laughing Graces, joining with the nymphs,
Pad the ground with tripping steps, while burning
    Vulcan visits spark-blown Cyclops' forge.

Now's the time to fit your head with shining herb
    and flower, now the un-froze earth gives forth;
Now's the time for offerings to sweet Pan
    In shadowy groves, a pyre of sweet ewe-lamb.

For pale Death, impartial, kicks the door
    of towered kings, and cottages of the poor;
The life so short, a longer hope is vain.
    Soon enough the creeping night overwhelms,

And Pluto's narrow house, with narrow door.
　　There you can't win first shot at the wine,
Nor run your eyes over charming Lycidas,
　　For whom all the boys are burning now,
　　For whom the girls will be burning soon enough.

The Pilgrim
(1.5)

What boy is it, slender among roses,
Tempts you now, spread round with perfume,
Holly? For whom do you bind raven tresses
Alone in your room,

With wicked carelessness? How many times
Will he weep for the fate the false gods spin,
With horror watch the waves break all confines,
And bear the proud dark winds?

Who holds you now, he sails a tranquil sea,
And thinks the loving calm will always last,
Ignorant how treacherous the winds can be,
Until he shrinks beneath the blast.

God help him who thinks you fair. As for me,
I've done my voyage, and on the temple wall
I've hung my dripping clothes, and by them, all
Shall know myself to be

A pilgrim, in for the long haul,
Of the strong god of the sea.

Winter

(1.9)

You see Mount Constance now, whitely glistening,
Douglas Firs on slopes, snow-bent with the weight,
Skykomish river bridged with frost, listening:

With good pine logs laid out on the grate,
melt down the binding cold, Iole, and pour
the wine, romano and crisp pears on the plate.

Spill some wine for the gods (because the floor
is ruined in any case), who scatter the seas
and winds, and yet tall trees remain as they did before.

Let what be tomorrow what may please
the gods. Each day's a profit. Let the boy
not spurn sweet love (though steep its fees)

nor the light foot of the dancers, while creeping gray
is absent from his blood, but find that place
in night's dark corners where whispers make their way,

where the rippling laughter of the girl betrays
that she might be at once both hunter and prey,
resisting, so that yielding shows more grace.

Carpe Diem

(1.11)

Don't look for it, Tony, 'cause they won't tell you—
unspeakable to tell—what end they're handing out
to you, to me. Don't read the paper through
the horoscope. Don't even think about

how many winters—maybe just this one?
or maybe just five more?—are left to us.
Better to let whatever shall be to come.
See how December-grey Pacific cuts

the cold, wave-pounded California shore?
Taste, and touch, listen, understand, my brother.
Even as we pluck these strings, here's still more
moments killing moments, each envying the other.

Plunder this day, nor add aught to our sorrows.
Leave for the kids all treacherous tomorrows.

The Ship of State
(1.14)

O frigate! Red-faced warship, where are you heading,
so eager for the tide? Where now, what seeking now?
    Quick, get back to port. Can't you see
    the oarlocks stripped of oars, the yards

are groaning, mauled by Iraqi Shamal, the dread
Simoom is shredding the lines, poor sailors splicing
    in the blast, your hull still battered
    from disremembered Monsoon rains.

There's not a sail still whole in all this ship, no god
who hears your call, however much you claim his favor,
    or boast your heart of oak (the tree
    most thunder-struck by vengeful Jove).

The handsome figurehead, the well-loved starry flag,
the painted taffrail, hard-pressed sailors do not trust.
    Unless you wish, like your fathers,
        to be a mockery for winds,

beware. You, who in my youth were but a headache,
and now are all too much my care, not lightly held:
    Try not this strait again, grinding
        between Scylla and grim Charybdis.

To Venus
(1.19)

Venus, that cruel mother of Love,
    and the wine-soaked son of Semele,
along with wanton Loudmouth (my own god)
    compels me to replenish my song
with love long past—

Still burning me, the flashing elegance of Holly,
    radiant as the marble shores of Lydia,
her bold brashness (welcome to me) still burns:
    her face too studied, too inconstant
in expression to be read or trusted,

her slender fingers, rapid as she ate,
    the rush of her rare laughter, the frank
declaring of her thought: "I'm bored." Or, hands
    in pockets, smiling when reappearing
after six miserable days: "Didja miss me?"

Venus, forsaking her native Cypress,
    runs me down like a deer,
and will not let me write about Iraq
    or Charlottesville, or anything to keep
me from this tired, still-burning theme.

Here, boys, here let's build a fire,
    an altar to our sad, mad, vengeful She.
Lay down the sage-bundles and rose incense.
    Perhaps, even through this paltry sacrifice,
She may become gentle, and kill these dreams

of sweet regret.

Ode to Joy
(1.22)

For him whose life is whole, unsullied by the scum
of past misdeeds, Toby, who has need
of weapons?—who, moreover, needs a gun,
    letting his hate feed?

Even down on Red Square, people getting shot
defying new tyranny, and thralls of president Tweet:
But whatever the danger, still are you not
    safer, without the heat?

Listen: Saturday, a huge brown bruin
ran off from me—armed only with a grin,
while wandering on a mountain trail, mooning
    over winsome ᚹ [3].

Now there's an omen you couldn't collect
even from Delphi, even from the Pythia
who, mazed by the mist of whispering cleft,
    advises ill to you.

---

3 ᚹ *wyn*, a character from the Germanic runic alphabet, meaning "joy."

Drop me in the middle of Mojave,
where Joshua trees gasp in the summer parch;
or Terafino, where the Spring rains
　　　blast through March;

Even Slab City, not fit for living thing,
a place beat hard, too near within
the wheels of Sun's chariot: still I'd sing
　　　of laughing, sweet-spoken Ᵽ.

Midnight on County Line
(1.23)

Like the white-tailed deer, Laurianne, you flee,
as if to seek your mother in the trackless hills,
frightened of the wind and wood—and me.

Yet here the fragrant summer night distills
sea spray upon your lashes, in scented dark,
while yielding to touch, the heart desire fills,

and I no tiger, pursuing but to crush your heart.
Here's only you and I, a bottle of wine, half-gone,
a blanket left by my thoughtful friend, the spark

of gold cast on the waves by the sinking moon.
Stop looking 'round for that silly girl, your friend:
Admit that you're in season for a man.

Mourning
(1.24)

What then? Even if you could pluck the strings
so well as when trees wept for Orpheus,
could that compel the blood back to the empty ghost,
whom, even now with horrid wand,

Mercury, not heedful to our wish to know the Fates,
has penned up among his black, quiet flock?
So hard—but then let patience be more easy,
since fixing it is forbidden.

The Witch
(1.25)

No more can you, while strutting down Sunset strip,
waylay the guy in purple silken shirt and fancy car
and, for a trick of your sweet lip,
buy fancy clothes on his dinar.

Your ready witchcraft wanes; no more can you
spell men as you spelled me. Your glamor warps:
That oblong agate ring I once knew
seems grave food, jarred beside a corpse.

We all are blasted by our age, but here's worse:
You, so flashing brilliant, though doubtless mad,
squander all—your art, your purse—
whimpering after the poppy seed,

shrinking to a shade in some desert shack.
The pity of it! Such rich magic that was yours,
pissed clean away, never to come back:
You, who used to tie her hair with stars.

Truth or Dare on Abrego Road
(1.27)

Quit throwing bottles! You think this is East LA,
or what? The drunken god's, above all, gentle:
Let's keep his service here, nice and quiet.

Liquor and guns—what cunt put those together?
Some Texas shithead. Chill, my brothers, down
on bended elbow, keep it mellow, keep it chill.

So now I have to take a swig—of what?
Mezcal? I'll beat you to the bottom, boy.
Of course I'll eat the worm, the fuck you think?

But first, my price. I've got my dare, and now,
the truth. Let's hear him tell us now: Who's Mark
got in his sights, who's made him shave his chin,

and wash his sheets? ('bout time) I wanna know,
and will not drink for other payment, I.
Look how he's blushing. Scared to say?

Come clean. It's not like you to be ashamed:
Your secret's safe when poured into our ears.
Your foolishness is always noble. Talk!

You must be joking. Her? Poor fish! You've made
a maelstrom to swim in, don't say I didn't warn you,
a burning log, fit for a better flame.

Give me that bottle. And let it not be said,
I didn't wish the guy a merciful release,
whom Perseus himself scarcely could set free.

The Singer's Prayer
(1.31)

Allow me this prayer, sweet Latona's son:
To savor with grace whatever's put up at the bar;
To not endure a senile age, nor a nasty one;
Nor never be so broke to lack a good guitar.

For "Daughter," My Guild D4 Guitar
(1.32)

She calls me. Grant me, only child of mine,
if ever on you I found some pleasing song
that friends might recall, late, over the wine,
let's prolong

tradition flowing down from golden-haired
Apollo, strumming on his tortoise shell:
Here in shadow where idle thoughts are shared,
help me tell

a song of California: cool in shade,
beneath live oak in panting summer heat,
a red-haired girl on Hopi carpet laid—
Let me greet

the wire and wood, the Sun God's best invention,
in glad company, or where sadness lingers,
when I pay you, Daughter, your due attention
with pleasured fingers.

War Songs

(2.1)

So once again you're writing about war:
The crimes, the lives degraded, ghostly hulks
who make a wretched life beneath some bridge,
the sickening lust for weapons, shared by both
elected swine and fools who voted them in.

When can we once again write comedy?
Be funny? Give the people what they want?

But still I hear the deafening trumpets' roar
filling every ear, some keen, too few offended,
still see the tough guy generals on display,
their faces not begrimed with desert dust.

What foreign shore's still lacking in our blood?
What ravaged field still can thirst for it?

Lest you withdraw for good, you impudent Muse,
from jokes and love songs, all my former craft,
seek with me, within Dionysian cave,
more friendly measures, in a lighter key.

The Dark Skiff
(2.3)

Equanimity, with business going bad,
a mind most steady—this you have to keep,
a tempered mind, even when winning against
Fortune, Angela: "We who are about to die—"

Why does white poplar join with the pine
to weave their boughs together in pleasant shade?
Why do headwaters run down from cliff-born springs,
tremble into rivers sliding ever down?

Let's order wine, and cheese, and have too-brief
rose petals spread upon our loving beds,
while all the ruck of business, age, the black thread
of third sister, the saddest, keep their distance.

The headland that you bought, washed by cold tides
on high de Fuca cliffs, where Hernan dreams
to build a pleasure dome, young hands will ply
to other purposes, and different pleasures.

No matter. Whether born to the silver spoon,
or plastic, blessed with a name as plain as dirt—
like Shaw, or Stein, or Taylor— all of us
shall fall alike to nothing-sorrowed Orcus,

gathering together, we whose numbers
all are turned, consigned to eternal exile,
picked by random lot in self-same tumbler,
awaiting on the shore the frail dark skiff.

Too Soon!
(2.5)

Too soon! So young, she's unwilling to pull
your wagon, not yet equal to the demand
of duty—doesn't know what it is, nor can stand
the weight of you, a sweating, grunting bull.

Your young filly's thoughts all run to the green
fields, where, eager, she longs to run with friends,
her coltish fellows, down to river's end,
to sport under willows, bowing to the stream.

Get rid of your desire for unripe fruit.
See how the many-colored autumn luster
paints the ripening vines, their livid clusters
sucking newness up from twisted root.

Of this be sure: one day she will desire
only you. Too late! Those years defiant Time
has cut from you, she adds to her, now in her prime.
What matter? Now Lila, with insistent fire

seeks you, would marry you. And her you like
a little better than Audrey, not so much
as Chloë, whose shoulder, bare and white, shines such
as moon on wave, bright splinters in dark night,

like lovely Jerrick, comely as a girl,
or me, for that matter, at age nineteen,
who, if dancing in a ring of girls was seen,
even by one who, wise, well-known to me had been,

had not known which was which: between boy and girl
flickering, with unbound locks and golden curls.

Laguna

(2.6)

O Kelly, though you swear I must remain
where all the names of rivers end in "ish,"
in this sweet, moody land of mist and rain,
I still could wish

on warm Laguna sands to end my days:
The turquoise skies at sunset, pale rose
the clouds that shelter curling waves—
or if truly I could choose,

a Santa Barbara porch, if I were rich,
where I once roughshod rode, with buccaneers
of beer, lords of loud guitars. But such
were younger years.

Laguna, then, where eucalyptus shades
old hippies painting in Plein-Aire oils,
bubbles stream from new-wet sand under wave,
salt-fresh smells,

the dolphins' spout in morning sun, and sweet
the grape coming down from Uncle Pat's domain,
nights of splintered fire, where moonlight streaks
black waves with white flame.

It's there that you—at least, I hope it's you—
must scatter, from some rented stern, after the end
of music, magic, end of all things new,
the ashes of your poet friend.

No Fear

(2.11)

What plots the mad jihadi dreams of,
in between the lopping of heads, and foul
debauchery with helpless stolen slaves,
God only knows.

Let's hope to confront those who believe in nothing,
but lawyer-like parse nature from a long-dead book,
with better wisdom, and love—but these seem lacking
anywhere I look.

But why the panic, Swab? The chaos we created
is still an ocean away; do what they can,
your comfy way of life is not at stake,
and costs but little.

Quit sweating at a backpack on a bus,
don't let the cops call it security when they club you,
and since when was this a homeland? I thought
it was America.

The rose through seasons varies in her glory,
nor does the moon, red in harvest, shine
always with one face. Your life less than these,
why fret, why whine?

Why don't we, sitting under this sycamore,
drink as we used to, when our young brows
were crowned with garlands, and we strode like gods
among the girls?

Bacchus dispels all care. So where's my waiter?
Have him bring us oysters, with horseradish,
and pints of pale ale, crisp on the tongue,
cold as frost.

And while you're at it, send a text
to Lydia, that encyclo— O no,
rather a deviant harlot—to hurry over

with her guitar inlaid with pearly vines;
pry her out of her dingy apartment
with promised wine.

The Eucalyptus Bough
(2.13)

In an evil hour they planted you, you wretch,
gnarled Aussie bastard, beneath my father's door.
For this you survived the blight, to fetch
a bough just past my ear—

one foot left and I'd be pudding for crows—
must have weighed sixty pounds and more,
and, not content to miss me with the blow,
stove in the windshield of my car.

He'd break the neck of his own father,
the gardener who planted you back in '64,
spray the inner chamber of his guest
with midnight gore.

To what and whom will harm us, never
do we show concern sufficient, nor
the vaguaries of timeliness do we ever
bargain for.

The fisher on the cold Alaskan strait
fears not the winch, though by the score
it kills him, but the dark wave, his fate
hidden elsewhere.

The flitting shadow of the Muj enrages
the tense marine, kicking down the door.
But it's with the silent IED he engages,
then fears no more.

How near was I to the black curtain,
where Mrs. D draped a swatch across her leg:
"Come on in, Crow; you're bier's awaitin',
Come tap the keg."

There Sappho sits among the honored shades,
with plaint of faithless girls among the crowd,
and Morrison and Bowie roam the glades
with song no longer loud.

There Seeger strikes the banjo, sings
the hardships of the sailor, the refugee,
the sorrow that the ceaseless warfare brings
to folk no longer free.

Why wonder that, by sad songs stupefied,
the shades forget their ancient enmity,
that even I, my gift for grudging now denied,
even forgive you, you stupid tree?

Amid soft music, even fretful Orion
forgets impulsive torment, nor thinks
to continue harassing the innocent lion
or the timid lynx.

Simple Things
(2.16)

It's rest the weary sailor prays for, caught
in ten-foot swell, the stars blacked out, the moon
ghosting silver through grey pale clouds.
Even the siccario, groomed

for ready slaughter, only aches for peace.
No purple murex dye, reserved for kings,
no marbled floors can bring release,
nor diamond ring,

from those tumultuous cares that wing
in silence under laquered ceilings of the rich,
not knowing from image or material thing
which is which.

He lives well who lives with little, who admires
his grandma's salt shaker, gleaming on his table
(hers also), whose sleep no sordid vain desire
can disable.

Why sell your life for lands in different suns?
The Cinque Terra look like Laguna to me.
Even if I fled my troubled country, and my home,
from myself how could I flee?

Grant me, Fate, one humble acre of land,
and the gentle spirit of ancient song—
that, and the scorn of the angry mob.
Let me live so long.

At the End of Lahey Street
(2.17)

Why exhaust me with your reasons?
If death takes you before me, not my fault,
nor God's (though someone's),
if the assault

of sick-sweet disease might take you,
with whom I lay in summer silence,
gazing at black sky, strewn
with flickering diamonds,

in a field down the street from my lover's house,
where we, smoke-strewn, debated questions
stoned kids care about,
now not even worth mention:

Whether Nothing is or Everything: who said
we weren't philosophers? You then could be
both wise, and kind (though sad),
compassionate, even witty—

I would talk to you again, but knocking at the door,
there's someone else living in the house,
that person is no more.
Now when Scorpius

rises in summer over steep Siskiyou,
as if lying in that distant field I turn,
reach out my hand to tell you,
but find you gone.

The Gentry
(2.18)

No ivory lines the rails
    of stairways in my house, no gold
mined by sweating backs
    in Africa forms pillars to hold
my humble roof.

And yet an honest fellow
    am I, and given to a kindly vein,
and sometimes even rich
    folk seek me out. Nor do I complain,
a pauper, of anything more,

not to the gods,
    nor to my powerful friend, who might
make life more lavish
    for one content, while day still lights
to work my Crown Hill plot.

One day nudges
    forth the next, and in the back
the day after that is shoved,
    and all moons only to wane do wax,
all time reduced to rubble.

And buying marble
    as you buy up the neighborhoods of the poor,
for countertops,
    you build and push your tenants from their doors,
the marble tomb not remembered.

Will you even build
    these paste-boards to the ever-rising tide,
razing solid homes,
    those driven out, their children at their sides,
cast loose on the urban jungle?

No more certain hall
    shall entertain the rich man than the high
estate of Pluto, hospitable one:
    The six-foot shroud will wind the pauper as nigh
as the one adept at deals.

What would you have more?
    Even bribed, not even shadowy Orcus
would release Tantalus,
    even as he raises, discharged from their workhouse,
the wearied poor.

To Bacchus
(2.19)

On distant cliffs I've seen him teaching
ancient rites—believe it, future ages!—
the lissome nymphs attending his preaching,
and pointed-eared sages.

Evoi! Weird old cry, untranslatable,
ushered from the trembling breast that's full
of him under whose rod, led from stolid stable
charges the meads like a raging bull.

Like wild Bacchantes, driven beyond reason,
let me be touched, as my face in the night,
lifted to the moon in the rainy season,
by his mad might,

so strong that Cerberus, innocent of your cup,
laid down his horns, and under your stride put
his tail, and kissed with threefold lip
your departing foot.

On Bird's Wings
(2.20)

No common wing shall carry me, transformed,
beyond the cities, far from anger's sway,
nor shall I be delayed
in flight to heaven, though tossed with storms.

It is not I, a simple kid from Canoga Park,
shall fly to meet the waters of the Styx
(not I, whom you picked
for your companion), as the mounting lark.

Even now my shanks are changed, absurd
mutation, my skin like ill-hung crêpe,
downy-feathered my nape,
same as my temples, snowy as a bird.

All too soon shall I, like the child
with wings of wax, fall hard into the sea.
Then shall I be
all changed, in flight through regions wild.

The director at rehearsal, a rainy Sunday,
tells the sleepy cast that Doctor Sean
is dead. Moving on.
Now get out there. While mourning, let's be funny.

Then let no dirge attend my corpse. Don't rave,
or raise indecent wail or complaint;
show restraint,
and grant no pointless tribute of a grave.

Rumor

(3.3)

The man who's honest, holding to the right,
Is never shaken by the howling cry
Rising in the street,

The tyrant's sneer, nor by the sight
Of men swearing what they know is a lie,
The Address supplanted by the tweet.

But these are not fit themes for my guitar.
Where are you going with this? Someplace worse,
You silly Muse, who urge me sing of war,
You, more apt for jocund verse.

The Battle of Jutland
(3.4)

Calliope, you epic muse, descend,
and on your fluted tongue true song relate,
heroic story for my brother, for my friend,
the night and years grown late.

Do you hear? Or do I, deluded, think I tread
the pleasant track beneath the trees, where waters
underflow, through some dream? Where blessed dead
memories emerge unshattered?

Beyond the border of Toluca Lake,
nurse to my youth, I walk behind my brother,
true admiral, whose name one day I'd take
to give another.

Down to the reedy river we would walk,
I and Patrick—a hero, by my belief.
And wearied by our play, the sun, his talk,
down on some fallen leaves,

beguiled by those fabulous doves of story
that haunt our childhoods like guardian angels,
I'd listen, while Admiral Pat, in all his glory,
recounted ancient battles:

How once off misty Skaggerak,
in hot pursuit of Hipper's German scouts,
steamed Beatty in the Lion, his flag,
on The Run to the South.

Here (said Pat) they ran, with Scheer to the south,
pelting northward fast as they could go,
while the greater British fleet from Forth's mouth
fanned out under Jellicoe.

The Germans lay far beneath the Lion's lee
all veiled in veering mist and smoke.
The British turned in order (Pat moving wood
on the grass as he spoke)

At extreme range, they opened fire with shells
the size of Model T's—and all the skies rained iron:
The Indefatigable (fatigable, after all)
decks pierced, expiring,

Queen Mary, beset by Derfflinger and Seydlitz,
as a doe is harried by the hounds.
Her magazine touched, she flew to bits,
sought deeper ground.

Q turret on the flagship crushed, then flooded,
Beatty surveys, still hours away from support.
"Something wrong with our ships today," he muttered.
"Chatfield, two points to port."

O muse of epic, and you of gentler skill,
by you am I raised, my brother and I, givers
of song and story, raised to brown Verdugo Hills,
and green LA River,

you whose gentle counsel joins with joy in the gift.
We know the limits of force, who sweat and strained
in making widgets for whatsits, all the long day shift,
that went somewhere on some warplane.

Force, unguarded by wit, sinks by its own weight.
Then too, power made temperate by control, the gods
steer into greater feats. Likewise they hate
strength of itself overawed.

Witness the hundred-handed what I say is true,
whose impiety earned them the Tartaean sorrow,
or ask Orion, known assailant of chaste lady Moon,
brought low by her virgin arrow.

Kids These Days
(3.6)

The sins of your fathers, though guiltless, young
Americans, you will atone for, believe me:
our idols all begrimed with reek,
filthy images that will not leave me.

When you know yourselves less than gods,
you rule. From this, every beginning, every end.
That forgotten, to this cowboy empire
every curse and cross they send:

Shame taught by sneering License pride,
Beauty sold to sordid Artifice,
Wisdom's place by Cunning's guile denied—
Brotherhood betrayed by Commerce' kiss.

Not like these are the kids out in the streets,
born to warfare unlike Caesar's own,
waving song like placards, wise in beats,
knowing just how far is Down.

What does the damned Time not diminish?
Not youth, though bodies like flowers decay;
These seem more apt (with more reason) to finish
winners, than I did, one day.

A Rite of Thanks
(3.8)

So what am I, unmarried, on the first
of March, about? With candles, frankincense,
I, to a homely altar made of turf,
with humble step advance,

disregard the strife that hovers like a bat
above our cities, all the fulsome tide
of bile flowing free. What can all that
mean to minds to virtue tied?

Suffer, Sherm, the lamps to be lit all night,
and have a couple of shots for friendship's sake;
Begone all noise, all talk of plebiscite.
Chaos can wait.

Be now a little heedless, whoever may resent.
For one day, be a private citizen and take,
forbearing caution, what the hour presents.
All serious things forsake.

To Lydia

(3.9)

While you found me pleasing,
desiring no other arms
about your shining shoulders,
I strode down the street
as if I ruled all of Persia.

While you burned for no one other,
and Lydia was not second to Chloë,
O Lydia, in honoring my name,
I walked the wild wood
with the arrogance of a viking.

Now Chloë holds the rights to me,
skilled on strings, wise in dance,
for whom I would not fear to die,
if proud Fate allows her to outlast me.

Still: what if Venus would return,
and gather those severed in a brazen yoke?
If Chloë, golden haired, should be cast out,
the door standing open to my Lydia?

Chloë, more fair than any star—
and you, as light as bobbing cork,
ill-tempered as the shameless sea:

I'd die just to live with you,
live just to love with you.

For Lonely Girls
(3.12)

For lonely girls, no time with Love to play,
or respite from the strict guardian's command,
or sweet red wine, to wash hard pain away.

The evil kid with deadly bow in hand
(and who is there that knows him could paint
his barb as other than a burning brand?)

makes your fair heart, Melissa, grow faint
when Marcus, fleet both horseback and on foot,
dips his dark shoulders, free from shirt's restraint,

in green water off of St. Anne's beach,
his narrow chin soft-downed like fresh-plucked peach.

The Bandusian Spring
(3.13)

O Piper's Creek, stream clear as glass,
qWàtub the Duwamps called you,
"dropping down," icy under alders,
cool harbor for so many:

The mason bees, hiving the apple orchard,
a hundred years old, at your northern corner;
and still-living salmon run, the lively smelt
flitting through the shadows

like ancient souls, big-eyed with the knowledge
of how the fog-fed rain of salmon flesh,
spread by bear and eagle on high basalt cliffs
built this rivered forest land.

And where the creek fans out to Puget Sound,
dispersed over fifty yards of rocky beach,
the smelt, as if in desperate race, on finny legs
skim across damp channels,

until one cannot tell: are they swimming?
Running? Fish or children? And all the time
the gulls, swooping down, determined murder,
catching up the fry.

The children come by with teachers, gathering up
the smelt in tiny hands, bear them from the creek
to the surf, and uncertain destinies,
smiling, having defended the weak.

Just Enough
(3.16)

Just as much as you refuse for yourself,
the more the gods will grant. Busted flat,
myself, I seek the camp of those desiring nothing,
deserter from the faction of the fat,

wealthy in contemptible things: an old fox skin,
a jar of arrowheads, two lamps of clay
formed on Jordan shore when spare Essenes
hid in caves arcane lore away,

a row of not-quite-first-rate guitars. Lord
am I more splendid that if I'd hoard
all the wealth gathered up in Yakima fields
by brown hands, poor amid great yields.

As long as water runs unleaded through the tap,
as long as my square hundred feet can bring up fruit,
I count myself more blessed than any Satrap
spending petrodollars teaching children how to shoot.

No hive gives me the lavender honey of Sequim,
nor do I crush my own Walla Walla grape;
I lead no nibbling sheep, as used to roam
on Malibu canyon hills, when I was young;

and yet, the worst of poverty is past me now;
and if I'd ask for more, you'd not deny to give.
My needs so small, the money goes far enough
for one who is at last content to live.

Incoming Storm
(3.17)

Hey Justin, though you're all dug in across
the bridge that binds new neighborhoods to old—
the new, when I was denizen, were dross,
now home to migrant gold,

and I exiled where Scandahoovians,
smelling of fish, and with cork heels shod,
once (some still) sailed out to Alaska rains,
hauling tons of cod—

Tomorrow (unless he lies, the aged crow,
my spirit) will bring the southwest storm in,
the streets all spread with boughs downed by the blow
(his caw is my warning).

Before it comes, get your guitar into its case.
Let your attendant spirit bring a log
for the fire. I'll take the middle, you the bass.
And yes, you can bring your goddam dog.

For My Garden
(3.18)

Gentle Pan, lover of nymphs who flee you,
welcome you are to wander
through the calm bounds of my small plot.

May you be kind to the fragile seedlings,
accosted by slug and snail,
for whom in traps I pour your offering of beer.

The starlings whirr and whistle in the firs,
The northern flicker whoops
on the tin roof of a nearby shed;

The scent of pine, blent with manure spread—
the country boy's perfume—
Grant that I might idle here all day,
delighting thrice to stomp the stubborn clay.

Fighting Over Mark
(3.20)

What danger you want to get into, Diego,
poking with your stick the papery nest
of the wasp: soon you'll be running scared,
a limp conqueror.

Don't you see, past the crowd of suitors
stammering something witty around young Mark,
her, fixing him with her eye, a lioness,
intent on her target?

A fine victory—if you could win it. Me,
I'll put my money on the other side.
Already filing her teeth, she approaches,
As sure as a bench-warrant

to be the one tonight to brush
his shoulders with the touch, like light breeze,
that caught up Ganymede from the fields
of well-watered Ida.

Vintage Bottle
(3.21)

You, like me born under Eisenhower,
whether you come bearing brawls
or bringing laughter, or the spur
to maddening love, or only sleep,
dusty green bottle
with fading label all in cursive French,

for whatever sake the Massic you hold
was gathered for serving out some grateful day,
let's drain you, since Stratmann orders
the white to be carried out to pair with fish.

That guy, howsoever he be soaked in po-mo slop,
will not turn up his Saxon nose at you.
Sheer madness, since even Venerable Foucault
was said to often warm his virtue with his wine.

With pleasant torment you provoke thought
slow to stir when unwined,
and by your counsel make unhid
solution of care for those that are wise,
deep secrets for us who are mad.

Mirthful laughing one, free one, wolfish wine!
You bring hope back to anxious hearts,
tooth and claw to the poor man's fight,
when, armed with you, he trembles not
at crowns of kings, or the clubs of racist cops.

Let freedom reign, and Venus, if she wills,
and all three sisters, pleased to grace our table.
Let the lamps shine out on all the garden,
while sun-chased stars flee across night's sables.

Pagan Girl

(3.23)

Only raise to her your upturned hands:
the moon, a sliver, birthing even now,
Wiccan Tara, one joss-stick for the land
and for the hearth-gods, slow

to anger: such suffices to protect
the tender seedlings from the hard hail's evil,
from him I hate above all other insects,
the pea-weevil.

Time was they fed the sacred double axe
more costly sacrifice, amid the oak and holly
fattening, near sacred Nemi, on the grass
of Alba. All we

must do requires no blood spilled savagely.
Quiet offering, the heads of little gods
crowned with brittle myrtle and rosemary,
an altar of green sod.

If pure the hand that greets the altar,
our dead, though angry, may bless us, as they ought.
Spared costly blood sacrifice, let us offer
clean cornmeal, grains of salt.

For the God of Wine
(3.25)

Where are you taking me, spirit rapt of wine?
    To what grotto, what grove, do you drive me
Swiftly, with new thought, strange mind,

Where I shall meditate, in whatever cave you hide me,
    A dream thought once, now thought anew,
As long as your spirit will abide in me,

Singing false pictures, picture something true?
    As the sleepy camper, stupefied at dawn,
Is mazed by Columbia Gorge, startled by the view

Of red rock columns, lit by rising sun,
    So shall I, hidden in some untrodden wood,
Sit mingling, 'til sound and sense are one.

For you, no trivial thing I'll sing for mortal good,
    You, whose followers, when devotion's hot,
Can uproot tall ash trees, tearing through the wood.

What sweet danger! To sing the wine-press god,
    Who crowns my temples, makes me rage
    In midnight rain the rapture of my age.

An Appeal to Venus
(3.26)

Long time ago, in my blossoming,
I served with glory in Love's campaigns.
Now, my weapons have done with war,
and my lyre I hang on the wall,

the left side, consecrate to Venus.
Here, right here set down the torches;
I here renounce the levers and crowbars
we used to break into Love,

and simply pray, goddess of Cypress
and Memphis, lacking Thracian snow,
that you lay the lash raised high,
just once, on proud Mari.

Europa
(3.27)

Not long before, gathering flowers in the meadow,
    fashioning crowns
for nymphs—now wave-tossed, seeing but shadow,

black canyons of surge, the silent stars,
    she wonders,
clinging, boldly terrified, to the barbarous horn:

"Now father, name of daughter, and piety
    all left behind!
conquered utterly by lust in frenzy.

"Where have I come, and why? Do I wake,
    and weep for shame,
Or do I sleep, and some empty phantom takes

"his way through ivory gates, a false dream
    to weave for me?
This strange beast, his breast as white as cream—

"Was it best to plunge into the deep sea's power,
    or in the meadow to remain,
Gathering up the unwilled Spring flowers?"

And cruel Love answers, laughing, with a nod,
    "You know yourself not,
O bride of the unconquerable god."

Like a River
(3.29)

You fret about the condition of the state,
and, worried, you fear for the city:
    What the new torch and pitchfork crew
    and their false prophet might do.

It's well that gods veil over future times
in misty night, and laugh when mortals are afraid
    beyond reason. Remember
    to sort what's in control

with equanimity—that's all you may command.
What's left over is just like a river,
    peaceful in midstream,
    smoothing rounded stones,

Until the mountain storm comes down, and strikes
the hollows with turned-up trunks, drowned flocks,
    the houses broken, people
    calling for help on rooftops,

until the waters quiet. The man content may say,
"I am alive. And tomorrow, let whoever deals
    the cards, send either black cloud
      or sunshine. Deal me in."

Fortune, glad in her savage business, and
obstinate in playing her shameless game,
    shifts her uncertain honors,
      now kind to me, now to another.

I love her while she lives with me. If she flies
with swift wings, damn her! What she's given, I resign,
    and wear what I had before I met her:
      my virtue, the poor man's dowry.

Love, Let Me Be
(4.1)

Your wars with me long halted, Love,
why now another attack? Let be!
I am not as I was in the hard reign of Holly.
Let be, savage mother of sweet Desire,
now sixty summers have come and gone.

Go vex Allan; though he's as old as I,
he'll be a sap for you and all you offer.
Your banner will be spread in his campaign,
in dancing steps of girls, bright of foot,
he'll build your altar where soft music rings.

Myself, neither woman or girl can now please.
No credulous hope for joy in mutual ease,
nor drinking deep with strangers in small hours,
way past weaving my long locks with flowers.

So why, Kate, why this tear upon my cheek?
Last week with you, my voluble tongue
could not shut up. And now, all silenced,
bereft, I meet with you only in dreams,

where now I hold you captured in my arms,
and now, in flight, pursue with desperate wing
through wooded glade, through rolling wave,
you, cruel thing.

Just Like Drusus

or There's Always One Nut at Shakespeare in the Park
(4.4)

Just as the roebuck fawn, tranced by the tit
of tawny mother in lush pasture, sights
(driving him from milk)
the lion, creeping slow, with focused scan,
and sees himself about to be taken:

So the drunken pig who's handing Abby shit,
and yelling "Hypocrites!" at us in tights
and pretend silk,
sees gentle Josh advancing, mild as any lamb,
though able—now intent—to cut some bacon.

Playing the Blues
(4.6)

The poet's god, the Sun, has given me life,
the name (a humble name) of poet, and art
of song, a life given less to fame than strife.
O Ian and Jenna, who are the Muses wards,

observe the Piedmont rhythm of my thumb:
one two, one two, and all the melody
is dancing, first and second strings among,
like Artemis, flitting through the wood for prey.

You, who duly sing the hymns of night
and Her who bodies forth the month's increase:
I leave to you to keep Art's ark aright,
to know her as Design, and yet Release.

and later, say you learned about the world
and art, when to my song, at three, you twirled.

Spring Again
(4.7)

The frosts are off the mantle: both I
and Earth are eager for becoming.

From off the hummocks, lain heavy down
with rye and vetch grown all last summer,

Sleeping all this winter, growing warm
in dark, worm-bearing loam,

I fling the burlap of long sleep, and wake
my little acre with seed and kiss.

The things we wish, we love, are not
immortal. The year and hour

That finally will snatch away the day
of our nourishing

Remains, as sure as the whiskered frost
has vanished in late March,

And apple-bearing Autumn bring fruit, and then,
and then, and then—

We, who know the story, shall sink down
where father, mother,

All the friends of youth, with all dreams,
are but shadow.

Who knows where the guardians of Time
will add any more todays?

You know as well as anyone, Whatley,
that they don't take money,

Music, or any kind of currency
to break the Lethean chains.

For Jeremy
(4.9)

Don't think that these shall die, these words
that I, the hermit poet of purple-dusk Cascadia,
    sing as companions of strings.

Helen was not the first to feel the heat
at the oiled locks and gold-spangled clothes
    of the Anatolian;

Many were strong after mighty-armed Achilles,
but all those heroes lie forgotten, because unsung
    by epic poet.

Virtue, concealed: no better than lazy, when you're buried.
So lucky you. Of you I won't be silent,
    beloved Jezzie.

So much smarter than me, friend in doubtful times,
enemy of deceit, distrustful of the smiling dollar,
    drawing all things to itself,

preferring what's honorable to what's easy,
less forgiving of the sheepish crowd, more tried
    by mad Conscience.

Not him possessing much you'd rightly call blessed,
but he more rightly takes the name who knows the use
    of the god's gifts,

grown skilled in bearing with hard poverty,
fearing shame more than death, nor for a friend,
    or a just cause,
      afraid to perish.

The Mirror
(4.10)

O cruel one, still flush with force within:
When down, all unexpected, shades your chin,
and those lush locks grow grey and thin,

You shall, with your most conscious self most missed,
ask why Age lacks Youth's knowledge, and desist
from such self-love as I, when I my mirror kissed.

He's Not Into You
(4.11)

There's a jar of wine here, nine years old,
Amy, in my garden, and ivy and parsley
for weaving garlands.

Crowned with these, you shine, the house
all gleams with silver vessels, and the altar
longs to be purpled.

Every hand is hurried, here and there
the girls run about with dishes, the boys
turning roasting spits.

And while we wait on these delights,
I've got to tell you (it's my birthday, after
all, I've got license for the truth):

I know you're hot for Telephus—not your type—
but anyway, some rich girl's nabbed him now,
holds him by a golden chain.

Remember Phaeton's wild ride among
the stars, and immortal Pegasus weighed down
by clumsy Bellerophon?

I hope you always follow what's fit for you,
thinking it wrong to hope for what is wrong,
even if allowed.

I know, easy for me to say, not to be loved
again by woman; learning verse instead,
desire melting into song.

In Ostia

(4.12)

Already the companions of the Spring:
the easy Southwest breeze, dwarf daisies
crowding through green grass, no more
do meadows stiffen with hoarfrost,
nor do the rivers roar
swollen with winter snow.

Amid pale pear blossoms at dusk, the thrush
trades babbling *arpeggii* with the flicker,
who answers with his single, puzzled note,
and from some hidden source, the scent
of jasmine finds me,
caresses, enshrines me.

The season makes me thirsty, Anders: Come,
leave your sea-cliff home and pleasant wife,
and walk the antique streets of Ostia with me,
and after plodding thousand-year old roads,
where rutted stones
oppress our feet, our bones,

we'll find some dive, near where Pompeii
still radiates the scent of fire and brimstone,
a close place, where the locals scream
at Naples football on the TV screen,
and you and I, unnoticed,
can discuss Rosaria, our hostess.

If such delights can win you, come on down.
Bring nothing, all we need is found
on the road, where we remember who we are,
where we first met. Don't give it too much thought:
Let's get in the car and drive.
Good time to be foolish, good to be alive.

Lyce and Chia

(4.13)

The gods have heard, Lyce, my prayer, that I
Might live to see you again, now in your croning:
Both you and I desire
Still with fire to stir up fire,

And I, all liquored up, once again ply
The strings and sing those songs that saw my dawning,
Lilting luridly on Sugar-E,
Who's not quite forgotten she knows me.

But you've improved with age—Your patterned gown,
Long dark locks in bound topknot, falling stray,
Eyes as crisp and black as night:
I wish I could, I wish I might

Be back in that room, on that night long gone,
Where I caught you dancing, on my way
To the can, with Chia (here
Tonight as well, drinking my beer).

That night, that long lost night, somehow I held
A scarf: as you two danced in that back room,
I walked in and lassoed you,
And, to laughter, in I drew

My clutch of laughing maidens. To break the spell
Of silence, first you I kissed, then (not too soon)
Kissed Chia. Then, nothing spoken,
You kissed Chia, all barriers broken.

O where has Venus flown, and where my comely face?
Old oaks she passes by, old bulls of yellow teeth.
What do I keep of him
Who every girl wished to win,

Whose speech was passionate fire? The trace
Of the firebrand, now thrown into relief
Of deep shadow, matches
The embers, fallen into ashes.

Epilogue: The Headstone
(3.30)

The carving's finished—not as burnished bronze
    so lasting, nor so steep as pyramids,
yet here no rain that may efface sweet sounds,
    no wild North Wind that song may keep hid,
nor endless tread of years, devouring flight
    of Time may hush these whispers in the night.

No victory over the goddess of no eyes
    do verses grant, and these but castles are,
of sandy filigree, who wait with small surprise
    between the mottled rocks upon the shore,
for song is but a moment—poised, but brief
    as is the swan-dive of the autumn leaf.

Poems are not stone, and here's no fame,
    that dies out finally as vestal's fire.
And yet the weave of thought and song give name
    to a shimmering clarity, enduring past the pyre.
So long as they invade the green-roomed wave
    with waxen boards, so long as fingers weave

sweet melody on beat-up old guitar,
       and northwest ridge is wrapped in silver mists,
and grey waves pound October's cloudy shores,
       I will be heard, in Spring when lovers kiss
in meadows of California oak, lacking rain,
       or Puget sun through purpling curtains strains,

not first to work the field of the Venusian bard,
       that pleasant man, but subtle Sapphic line
to bend to west coast climes, plain-spoken words.
       If gracious thanks and pleasure so be mine,
Take these, whether by dancing or lamenting led,
       Melpomene, and set bay laurel on my head.